Friends
No Matter What
So Glad We Stick Together

Artwork by
Debbie Cook

HARVEST HOUSE PUBLISHERS
EUGENE, OREGON

Friends No Matter What
Copyright © 2004 by Debbie Cook
Published by Harvest House Publishers
Eugene, Oregon 97402

ISBN 0-7369-1309-2

Original artwork © Debbie Cook. Licensed by Looking Good Licensing, Washington, CT. For more information regarding artwork featured in this book, please contact:

Looking Good Licensing
15 North Sawyer Hill Road
Washington, CT 06777
(860) 868-1075

Design and production by Koechel Peterson & Associates, Inc., Minneapolis, Minnesota

Harvest House Publishers has made every effort to trace the ownership of all poems and quotes. In the event of a question arising from the use of a poem or quote, we regret any error made and will be pleased to make the necessary correction in future editions of this book.

Unless otherwise indicated, Scripture quotations are from the Holy Bible, New International Version®. NIV®. Copyright © 1973, 1978, 1984 by the International Bible Society. Used by permission of Zondervan. All rights reserved. Verses marked NLT are taken from the *Holy Bible*, New Living Translation, copyright © 1996. Used by permission of Tyndale House Publishers, Inc., Wheaton, IL 60189 USA. All rights reserved.

All rights reserved. No part of this publication may be reproduced, stored in a retrieval system, or transmitted in any form or by any means—electronic, mechanical, digital, photocopy, recording, or any other—except for brief quotations in printed reviews, without the prior permission of the publisher.

Printed in Hong Kong.

04 05 06 07 08 09 10 11 12 / NG/ 10 9 8 7 6 5 4 3 2 1

To My Friend:

_____

With Love:

_____

Walking with a friend in the dark is better
than walking alone in the light.

Helen Keller

No Matter What, We'll Always Be Friends

We've been through
a lot together, you and I.
And beyond the happiness
and the tears that
have been shared
comes something else...

It's a connection that
will always be there between us.
No matter where we go
or how much time passes,
you and I will always,
in a very special way,
remain together in spirit,
and that knowledge
is cherished by me
as the one thing that must never change.
In a world of constant transition,
I pray that what we feel
towards one another
will always stay the same.

— Collin McCarty

The happiest business in all the world
is that of making friends,
And no investment on the street
pays larger dividends,
For life is more than stocks and bonds,
and love than rate percent,
And he who gives in friendship's name
shall reap what he has spent.

Anne S. Eaton

There's a miracle of friendship
that dwells within the heart,
And you don't know how it happens
or where it gets its start…
But the happiness it brings you
always gives a special lift,
And you realize that friendship
is God's most perfect gift.

Author Unknown

And others—others go farther still, and move outside
humanity altogether. A place, as well as a person, may
catch the glow. Don't you see that all this leads to
comfort in the end? It is part of the battle against
sameness. Differences, eternal differences, planted by
God in a single family, so that there may always be
colour; sorrow perhaps, but colour in the daily grey.

E. M. Forster
Howard's End

For delays and hindrances may bar the wished-for end;
A thousand misconceptions may prevent
Our souls from coming near enough to blend;
Let me but think we have the same intent,
That each one needs to call the other, "friend!"

Amy Lowell

I must do as you do? Your way I own
Is a very good way, and still,
There are sometimes two straight roads to a town,
One over, one under the hill.

You are treading the safe and the well-worn way,
That the prudent choose each time;
And you think me reckless and rash to-day
Because I prefer to climb.

Your path is the right one, and so is mine.
We are not like peas in a pod,
Compelled to lie in a certain line,
Or else be scattered abroad.

'Twere a dull old world, me thinks, my friend,
If we all just went one way;
Yet our paths will meet no doubt at the end,
Though they lead apart today.

You like the shade, and I like the sun;
You like an even pace,
I like to mix with the crowd and run,
And then rest after the race.

I like danger, and storm, and strife,
You like a peaceful time;
I like the passion and surge of life,
You like its gentle rhyme.

You like buttercups, dewy sweet,
And crocuses, framed in snow;
I like roses, born of the heat,
And the red carnation's glow.

I must live my life, not yours, my friend,
For so it was written down;
We must follow our given paths to the end,
But I trust we shall meet—in town.

Ella Wheeler Wilcox

Once the package of friendship has been opened, it can never be closed. It is a constant book always written, waiting to be read and enjoyed. We may have our disagreements. We may argue, we may concern one another. Friendship is a unique bond that lasts through it all.

Author Unknown

The rain may be falling hard outside,
But your smile makes it all alright.
I'm so glad that you're my friend.
I know our friendship will never end.

Robert Alan

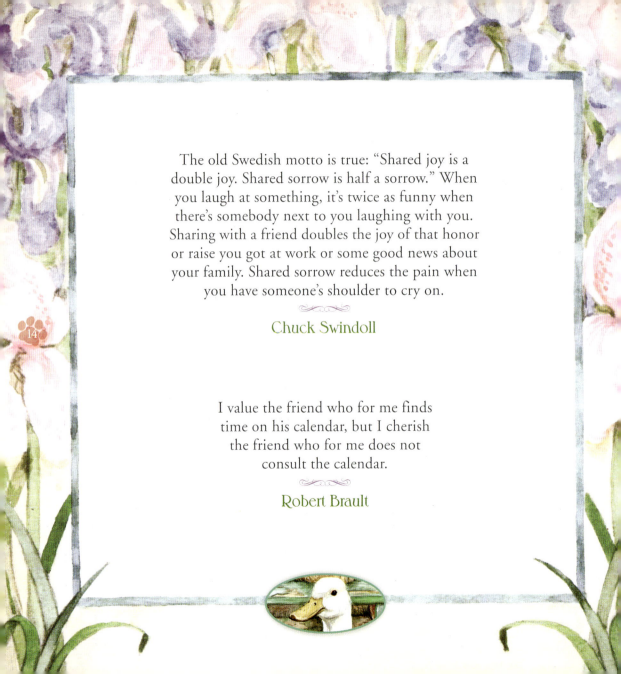

The old Swedish motto is true: "Shared joy is a double joy. Shared sorrow is half a sorrow." When you laugh at something, it's twice as funny when there's somebody next to you laughing with you. Sharing with a friend doubles the joy of that honor or raise you got at work or some good news about your family. Shared sorrow reduces the pain when you have someone's shoulder to cry on.

Chuck Swindoll

I value the friend who for me finds time on his calendar, but I cherish the friend who for me does not consult the calendar.

Robert Brault

Friendship, "the wine of life," should, like a well-stocked cellar, be continually renewed; and it is consolatory to think, that although we can seldom add what will equal the generous first growths of our youth, yet friendship becomes insensibly old in much less time than is commonly imagined, and not many years are required to make it mellow and pleasant. Warmth will, no doubt, make a considerable difference. Men of affectionate temper and bright fancy will coalesce a great deal sooner than those who are cold and dull.

James Boswell

A friend is one before whom
I may think aloud.

Ralph Waldo Emerson

If a man does not keep pace with his companions,
perhaps it is because he hears a different drummer.
Let him step to the music which he hears,
however measured or far away.

Henry David Thoreau

One lesson we learn early,
that in spite of seeming difference,
men are all of one pattern.
We readily assume this with our mates.

Ralph Waldo Emerson

Because we're different, we can have the fun of
exchanging worlds, giving our loves and excitements
to each other. You can learn music, I can learn flying.
And that's only the beginning. I think it would go
on for us as long as we live.

Richard Bach

A friend loves at all times,
and a brother is born for adversity.

The Book of Proverbs

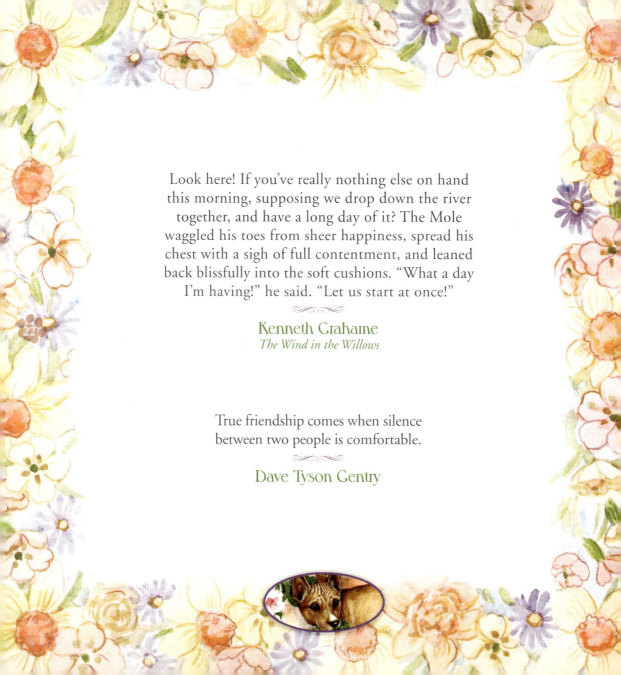

Look here! If you've really nothing else on hand this morning, supposing we drop down the river together, and have a long day of it? The Mole waggled his toes from sheer happiness, spread his chest with a sigh of full contentment, and leaned back blissfully into the soft cushions. "What a day I'm having!" he said. "Let us start at once!"

Kenneth Grahame
The Wind in the Willows

True friendship comes when silence between two people is comfortable.

Dave Tyson Gentry

Everyone who has ever done a kind deed for us, or spoken one word of encouragement to us, has entered into the make-up of our character and of our thoughts, as well as our success.

George B. Adams

Your friendship's like a touch of spring that warms and brightens everything.

Author Unknown

It is one of the severest tests of friendship to tell your
friend his faults. So to love a man that you cannot
bear to see a stain upon him, and to speak painful
truth through loving words, that is friendship.

Henry Ward Beecher

What is a friend? I will tell you…
it is someone with whom you
dare to be yourself.

Frank Crane

A Friend Like You

There's lots of things
With which I'm blessed,
My problems have been few,
But of all, this one's the best:
To have a friend like you.

In times of trouble
Friends will say,
"Just ask, I'll help you through it."
But you don't wait for me to ask,
You just get up and do it!

And I can think of nothing more
That I could wisely do,
Than know a friend,
And be a friend,
And have a friend like you.

Author Unknown

From quiet homes and first beginning,
Out to the undiscovered ends,
There's nothing worth the wear of winning,
But laughter and the love of friends.

Hillaire Belloc

A true friend is someone who
thinks that you are a good egg even
though he knows that you are
slightly cracked.

Bernard Meltzer

My friend, if I could give you one thing, I would wish for you the ability to see yourself as others see you. Then you would realize what a truly special person you are.

Barbara Billingsly

They were developing one of the little differences, or quarrels, that composed the very texture of their friendship.

Booth Tarkington
Penrod and Sam

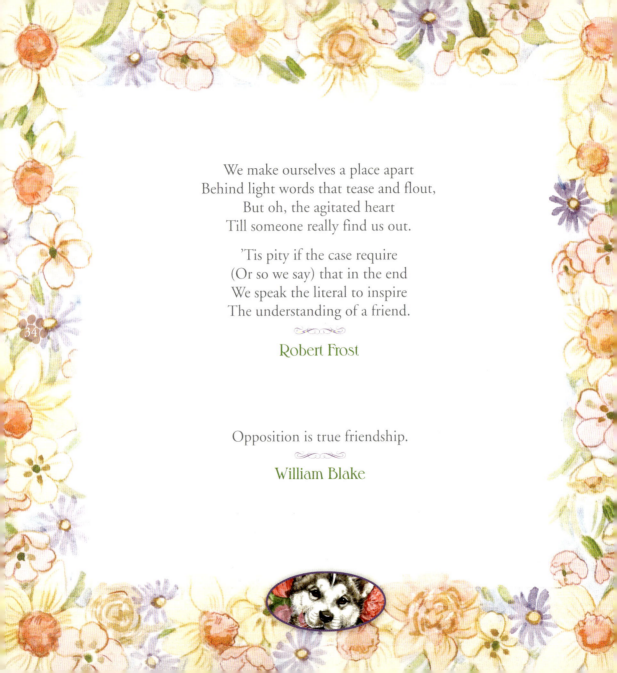

We make ourselves a place apart
Behind light words that tease and flout,
But oh, the agitated heart
Till someone really find us out.

'Tis pity if the case require
(Or so we say) that in the end
We speak the literal to inspire
The understanding of a friend.

Robert Frost

Opposition is true friendship.

William Blake

She now became quite happy. The motor-car ran on, the afternoon was soft and dim. She talked with lively interest, analyzing people and their motives…the reactions were all varied in various people, but they followed a few great laws, and intrinsically there was no difference…They were all essentially alike, the differences were only variations on a theme.

D.H. Lawrence

Truth springs from argument amongst friends.

David Hume

A friend drops their plans when you're in trouble, shares joy in your accomplishments, feels sad when you're in pain. A friend encourages your dreams and offers advice—but when you don't follow it, they still respect and love you.

Doris Wild Helmering

A friend is one who knows us, but loves us anyway.

Jerome Cummings

No Better Friend

The day is warm with sunshine and
The sky is extra blue
Because in all the world I have
No better friend than you

Because you always greet me with
A kindly word and smile
And in a dozen different ways
You make my life worth while

You comfort me whenever I
Have any fears to hide
And when my heart is sad I know
That you are at my side

I look to you for counsel and
The courage that I need
As well as inspiration for
My every daily deed...

And all the stars are silver-bright
When night is young and new
Because I know in everything
I can depend on you.

James J. Metcalfe

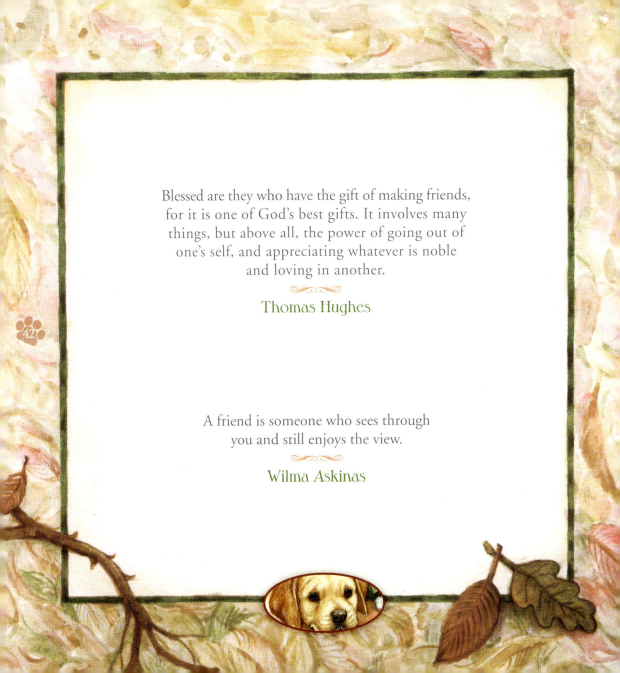

Blessed are they who have the gift of making friends,
for it is one of God's best gifts. It involves many
things, but above all, the power of going out of
one's self, and appreciating whatever is noble
and loving in another.

Thomas Hughes

A friend is someone who sees through
you and still enjoys the view.

Wilma Askinas

The finest kind of friendship is
between people who expect a great
deal of each other but never ask it.

Sylvia Bremer

As iron sharpens iron, a friend
sharpens a friend.

The Book of Proverbs (NLT)

Little friends may prove
great friends.

Aesop

Don't walk in front of me,
I may not follow.
Don't walk behind me,
I may not lead.
Just walk beside me
and be my friend.

Albert Camus

My best friend brings out
the best in me.

Henry Ford